Unspotted

One Man's Obsessive Search for Africa's Most Elusive Leopard

Unspotted
One Man's Obsessive Search for Africa's Most Elusive Leopard

Justin Fox

Annorlunda*Books*

Contents

CHAPTER ONE

A magnificent obsession

Quinton Martins is mad. Not in some superficial, mildly nutty way, but rather with a deep and abiding insanity. His madness began in 2003 when he became obsessed with the idea of finding the near mythical Cape Mountain Leopard. Most Capetonians know they exist—their tracks are occasionally spotted in the mountains and a farmer kills one every few years, to much public consternation – but no-one ever actually *sees* them. So really, they only half exist, occupying a place on the borders of public mythology.

In 2003 Quinton started looking for the elusive cat in the Cederberg mountains. He would go for weeks at a time, hiking alone in their remoter parts, searching for any sign of leopard. His passion grew into a master's, then a doctoral, thesis. He poured all his time and money into finding the cat. Sometimes he'd lug a backpack filled with 16 cameras high into the berg to set up camera traps with infrared sensors. A week or two later he'd return to retrieve the film (there were only 36 shots to a roll) and set the traps in new positions. For months there were only blank film strips, or shots of small, non-descript mammals. Then one day he was in his local camera shop collecting photos and, as usual, he idly asked if there'd been any shots of cats in the latest batch of film.

"Ja, I think there's a nice one of a spotted kitty," said Zelda, the shop assistant.

It was as though a bolt of lightning had struck Quinton. Before he was fully aware of his actions, he'd vaulted over the counter and run through to the back room. Sure enough, it was a male leopard. He was destined to become M1, the first in a long line of cats that would consume Quinton's life.

It was nine months before he actually glimpsed his first leopard and another year before he captured and collared one. He ran out of money and sold everything, including his car, to keep the research going. He'd have to hitchhike from Cape Town to the berg and do his research on foot, covering thousands of miles in the mountains in temperatures that were well below freezing in winter and as high as 116°F (47°C) in summer. He carried no tent, just an old sleeping bag. When it snowed, he sheltered in a cave or rocky overhang. Madness.

I, too, have a thing for leopards. I wanted to meet Quinton... and, hopefully, one of his spotted friends.

CHAPTER TWO

Into the wilderness

I drove up the N7 from Cape Town one spring morning when wildflowers lined the road through the undulating Swartland; then up over the Piekenierskloof Pass towards the grey ramparts of the Cederberg, home to Quinton and his leopards. After the orange orchards of Citrusdal, I took the Algeria turn off and crossed the chattering waters of the Olifants River on a causeway. This is the symbolic entrance to the most beautiful mountains in Africa.

I stopped and got out to drink from a stream fringed with white sandbanks. Before me stood Grootberg's ochre buttresses, the berg's main portal. The road snaked into the mountains between slabs of sandstone towards a saddle in the clouds, each ridge leading me higher and deeper, past Algeria, over Uitkyk Pass and finally into the lovely Driehoek Valley. The floor was covered in sedges and marshes, the walls with boulders and protea bushes.

I was now in the heart of the Cederberg Wilderness area, 175,000 acres of mountainous terrain, rich in fynbos and home to the rare and endangered Clanwilliam cedar tree and snow protea. Formations of Table Mountain sandstone stretched into the distance in a series of peaks. This alpine vastness is still frequented by smaller wildlife such as Grey Rhebok, Klipspringer, Honey Badger, Caracal, Cape Fox, porcupine, and Cape Clawless Otter, while raptors such as Black Eagle and Jackal Buzzard circle in the thermals overhead. The streams are home to the richest variety of fish south of the Zambezi, most of them endangered. The prettiest of these is the Doring Fiery Redfin, with its sleek spotted body and scarlet fins, like a cross between a leopard and a daisy.

The Cederberg's allure is enhanced by its rich human history. These mountains were once the realm of San hunter-gatherers (also known as Bushmen) and possess a staggering wealth of rock art dating back 8,000 years. Indeed, this is the Louvre of the Cape. Some of the most famous of the paintings, such as those of the ghostly rain elephants – a row of ochre pachyderms thought to be a rainmaking site of shamans – are found at the Stadsaal rock formations, close to where I would be staying. The San were the original inhabitants of southern Africa and thrived in the Cederberg region, hunting antelope and smaller game, until they were pushed out, first by Khoikhoi herders, and later by white settlers. Today, the only large groups of remaining San can be found in and around the Kalahari Desert.

The Cederberg mountains, Western Cape.

I booked a hut on Driehoek Farm and brought along enough provisions for a lengthy spell of self-catering, which, for me, means lots of *braaiing* (barbequing), so the vehicle was essentially full of wood and meat. A farm road brought me to a cluster of buildings, some thatched and whitewashed in the Cape manner, loosely arranged around a green commonage. Sheep filled a field, a vineyard clung to the slope and the battlements of the central berg rose up on all sides. It was ruggedly idyllic. A pack of dogs, led by a white Labrador, bounded up and escorted me to the reception room. We passed an inflamed male turkey, gobbling appreciatively and ogling a dowdy female. He made a valiant attempt to mount her, but she would have none of it. The Labrador barked encouragement while I knocked on the door. It was opened by Lizette du Toit, the farmer's daughter. She signed me in, handed over the key to my hut and we got chatting about leopards.

"Farmers used to set gin traps to kill predators, but with Quinton around things have changed at lot," she said. "You must ask him about Houdini, the old leopard that took 15 of our sheep and my dad wanted him *dead*."

Lizette told me that Driehoek was established in 1832, making it the oldest farm in the Cederberg, and had been in the Du Toit family for five generations. She showed me a selection of the wines whose grapes came from some of the highest vineyards in South Africa. I was given a map and she pointed out a number of walks on the farm and adjacent mountains.

"Have you ever seen a leopard?" I asked.

"Ag, I've seen Max, our big male, a couple of times in my life, but these cats are *vrek* (extremely) difficult to spot. Good luck!"

She directed me to a hut a long way down a farm track in a stand of poplar and oak trees, all still leafless up here in the cold alpine air. A few empty caravans stood marooned in the campsite, like upmarket shacks. My accommodation was a wooden, open-plan affair half encircled by large boulders and a dry stone wall that dated from the 1800s. Out front was a tea-colored stream wending through the reeds; beyond lay the serrated foothills of Sneeuberg, stepping away in stony ridges towards the skyline. Behind my hut stood the squared-off monolith of Tafelberg, towering above the farm. It was a handsome spot.

The heater was on in the room, despite the bright sunshine. It was going to be bitterly cold at night. I began to stack my provisions on the counter: *wors* (sausage) and chops, plonk red wine, chips, chocolates, spaghetti and bolognaise in a jar. I hadn't finished unpacking when I heard a vehicle pull up outside. A tall figure with a floppy hat and spectacles stood on my *stoep* (porch) stomping the dust off his boots. "So, you ready to bag a leopard then?" said Quinton, rubbing his stubbly chin.

"Sure!" I said.

"Good, let's go set some traps."

Quinton was dressed from head to toe in sponsored gear. He had a web of crow's feet in the corners of his eyes, no doubt from years of staring at the sun-bleached landscape that hid his elusive cats. We climbed into *Witblitz*, his Land Cruiser, which was branded with stickers from a host of sponsors, including the rather appropriate Leopard's Leap Winery. The logo of the Cape Leopard Trust, of which Quinton is the founder and project manager, was emblazoned on the driver's door.

"We couldn't keep the trust going without sponsors," said Quinton as we bounced through the campsite. "But the bloody vehicle manufacturers won't give me a thing. Their 4x4s are carving up the landscape and they're too miserly to help with a project aimed at protecting the environment. Bastards." He chuckled. "It's not just sponsors we want. Volunteers too. I just need to make a quick stop and say hi to a retired couple up here helping me out. They're monitoring the transmitters on two traps I've set in the valley."

We pulled up beside a caravan parked in a glade of oak trees a few hundred yards upstream from my cabin. Garth emerged from the tin igloo.

"No luck, Quinton, I've been checking every hour." Garth was a bald, cheerful man and carried a Chestnut-fronted Macaw on his shoulder. Gracie concurred with a loud squawk. "Oh, she's such a clever girl. Wants to be involved in everything, don't you Gracie, even chasing after big kitties." The green bird ran its head up and down Garth's chin to the man's obvious delight. He scratched his little friend's head with a practiced forefinger.

"She was abused as a chick before we got her," said a pink-track-suited Lorraine, emerging from the caravan. "Now she only loves Garth. So possessive over him. Doesn't like women at all, not human ones anyway." She sounded miffed at having been usurped by a bird. "But you've at least learnt to poop on command, haven't you Gracie?"

The bird cocked its head.

"Poop, Gracie, poop," said Garth dotingly, directing her tail away from his shirt. "It's better that she poops out here and not in the caravan or on me."

21

"It brings good luck, you know," said Lorraine, trying to sound enthusiastic.

"I'm not sure how much more good luck I can handle," said Garth with a long-suffering smile.

"Maybe good luck turns bad if you get pooped on too many times," chirped Quinton.

"Oh no, it's always good luck if it's from Gracie," said Garth.

"Anyway, better be going. We'll take the receiver and give you a few hours off duty."

As Quinton pulled away, we could hear Garth and Lorraine saying 'poop, poop, poop' and Gracie calling after us 'bye, bye, bye.'

"Such a nice couple," said Quinton. "They've volunteered to sit here next to a receiver for a week, just waiting for the signal to change, which tells us a trap has been sprung. Without folks like them, our organization couldn't function."

As we drove up the valley, Quinton chatted about the Cape Leopard Trust. By 2004 his savings had run out, and it looked as though the research would have to be abandoned. Then a local farmer, Johan van der Westhuizen, asked to see him in his office in Cape Town. He asked Quinton to explain his research in minute detail. Johan was so impressed he handed over a check for R15,000 (roughly $1200).

"That cash injection allowed me to keep going," he said. "Our first leopard, M1, was named Johan."

Quinton's research soon led him to the conflict between humans and animals — the region had once had the greatest predator-farmer conflict in the Cape, with up to 17 leopards killed annually — and his focus began to shift. He felt strongly that leopards were being killed or relocated unnecessarily. If you eliminated a 'problem animal' other leopards simply moved in to contest for the vacant range, and this could cause even more trouble. Quinton wanted to find solutions that didn't involve culling. A simple research project was not enough.

That's when the idea of a predator-conservation trust came about. Fundraising events were held and money started coming in. The program grew and was extended to other parts of the Cape. Today, there are leopard projects running in the Boland mountains north-east of Cape Town, in Namaqualand on the West Coast and in the Gouritz region along the southern coast of the Western Cape.

"The biggest threats to the Cape Leopard are habitat loss, persecution, and disease," said Quinton in his laconic drawl, avoiding a protruding root that lay in the road like a fat python. "It's only through long-term research over decades that we can truly understand what affects the population. To see the big picture we'll also need to do ancillary projects on the leopards' prey, such as dassies (rock-rabbits) and klipspringers."

He explained that the board of trustees comprises eminent scientists, businesspeople, and conservationists. Apart from various leopard projects, the work of the trust includes a comprehensive genetic analysis, which will determine whether Cape leopards form a unique genetic unit or subspecies. Solutions to human-animal conflict are being sought through scientific research and empowering farmers and local communities, as well as by encouraging eco-tourism and running education programs.

Quinton took a right turn down a track that was closed to the public. The vehicle bounced over boulders like an inebriated frog.

"I first became interested in leopards while tracking them on foot in Londolozi Game Reserve," continued Quinton. "After a few years working as a ranger I decided to study again and ended up at the University of Cape Town doing zoology. During varsity holidays, I came hiking in the Cederberg and started to notice leopard tracks. Farmers told me about the problems they were having with leopards, but no one I spoke to had ever seen one. I discovered there was hardly any research on them at all. It was an ideal opportunity. A challenge, really.

"There's something special about these particular cats. I used to have up to six sightings of leopards a day in places like South Luangwa in Zambia, but here it's a massive challenge. To me, they represent this incredible wilderness so near Cape Town. You never see them. But they are here. If they were easy to spot they'd all have been killed long ago. They're such elusive, ghost-like creatures.

"I initiated the research project and funded it myself. We started getting sightings and then began trapping. My best encounter was in a remote *kloof* (gorge) on the eastern, Karoo side of the berg. It was a really tough hike to get in there. I was busy setting up a camera station next to a river when I heard a leopard vocalizing close by. It's an unmistakable rasping sound. You never hear that here. I thought the leopard might be coming along the path, so I hid a little way up the slope.

"Then I heard the vocalizing *right* below me in a riverine thicket. I scanned the bushes with my binoculars. Nothing. Lowering my binocs to get a broader perspective, I saw a little movement out the corner of my eye. Slowly I turned my head and there she was, peeping around a rock and staring at me, about 25 feet away. She had this absolutely perplexed look on her face. What the hell is this thing? I slowly moved my hand to my camera and she watched its progress intently. I raised this crappy digital point-and-shoot, pressed the trigger and '"poof"', she was gone. It's so isolated back in those *kloofs* there's a good chance she'd never seen a human in her life before. What a privilege, man, what a privilege."

The track petered out and the going got rougher. We crossed a river, drew to halt beside a large boulder and got out. Before us was a scene suggestive of a slaughterhouse. A grysbok hung upside down from a hook on the rock, its stomach slit open, blood dripping from nose and mouth. Heads and limbs of various animals lay scattered about. The stench was overwhelming.

Quinton pointed out the invisible trap. Sticks and bushes had been arranged so that there was only one easy way to reach the suspended buck. Quinton checked the foot-loop snare while I stood at a distance trying not to throw up. "The grysbok is road kill," explained Quinton. "The other body parts are offcuts from an abattoir."

Once he'd checked and reset the trap, we headed on foot up Uilsgat Kloof along a path used by F10, also known as Spot, a female leopard that frequented the valley. Quinton carried a backpack with trapping paraphernalia, which included a mallet and a number of metal stakes. The sun was low and we moved in and out of icy shadows. I realized I should have brought a jersey. We passed a second trap, right in the middle of the path. A red flag and signs warned people to keep clear. "I've asked Cape Nature to close this area to the public," said Quinton. "Hikers are such a pain. They don't read the notices, or if they do, the buggers come and snoop around, triggering the snare. They're clueless."

Quinton was looking for a suitable place to set another trap. As we headed further up the path I noticed that my companion had, almost imperceptibly, begun to change. His gait was somehow different, his body slightly hunched. Quinton seemed more alert, more twitchy. He stopped often, looking at the path with a cocked head. Thinking like a leopard?

"Here, this is the place," he said at last, lowering his backpack and taking the spade I'd been carrying. He dug a square hole, levered a foam base into position and laid the trap over the top. It comprised a simple foot plate, with a trip and spring fastened to a wire noose that would tighten around the animal's paw. The wire was thick and smooth so as not to hurt the cat. It was attached to a bungee cord so the leopard's yanking would not injure or break a limb. Quinton taped over any rough areas on the wire and cleared all stones and sharp sticks in the immediate vicinity so the creature would not injure itself as it thrashed about trying to extricate its paw. He carefully set the spring and attached a transmitter. The contraption was secured with long metal stakes driven into the ground by a mallet. It was imperative that a leopard be prevented from breaking free and heading into the hills with the trap attached to its leg.

"Aren't these snares just like the wire ones set by poachers?" I asked through chattering teeth.

"Similar. It's actually a more effective and safer method than the cage traps we used to employ. Animals picked up more injuries trying to force their way out of the cages. As long as we get to them soon after the trap is sprung, wire snares are okay. That's why the transmitters have to be monitored at all times."

He showed me how to set up a transmitter and how, as soon as the magnetic connection was severed, it started sending an altered signal. The volunteers at Driehoek would then call Quinton on a satellite phone and he'd race to the trap. If indeed a leopard was caught, rather than a blundering hiker, he'd phone the nearest vets, who were permanently on standby and could be there within two hours to dart the animal. A collar would then be fitted and measurements, tissue and whisker samples taken for DNA analysis. The cat would also be weighed, its age determined by teeth coloration and wear, and its general condition assessed.

Once fitted with a GPS collar the animals could be tracked around the clock and Quinton was gathering valuable information from the data downloaded. During the period of his PhD research he'd managed to trap and collar 13 leopards and had gained considerable insight into their movements, diet, and habits.

"Where did you catch your first cat?" I asked.

"It was on Driehoek farm in August 2005," he said, pushing back his floppy hat and wiping the sweat from his forehead. "We'd been trying to get him for three months. His name was Houdini, for good reason. By that stage I was already nearly two years into my research and had not yet had a proper, close encounter with a leopard. Houdini had been nailing sheep throughout the valley, but I convinced the farmers to give me a chance at nabbing him. That cat was a sly one. Eventually we lured him with a sheep carcass, but he escaped from the first trap. We reset it and caught him a week later. Again, he escaped. It took another five weeks before we finally got him."

Once he'd finished preparing the trap, Quinton arranged his camouflage and subterfuge devices. I was so cold I needed to bounce up and down to keep the blood circulating. Quinton ignored me as he covered his contraption with sand. This couldn't be done with a tell-tale human hand, so soil was sifted through a colander and sprinkled over the snare. Next, he cut foliage and planted it in a manner that would lead a leopard into the trap. Sticks were laid to encourage the cat to assume a particular stride and place its paw in exactly the right spot. Quinton was down on his hands and knees, head to one side, staring skeptically at the trap. He raised his front paw a little, hesitating, then adjusted a twig. He looked decidedly feline. If you narrowed your eyes, you could almost see his spots. Taking a few paces on all fours he slunk into the trap, all but triggering the snare around his wrist.

Quinton Martins setting up a trap that comprises of a simple foot plate, a trip and spring fastened to a wire noose that will tighten around the leopard's paw.

"The data we've been collecting can be used to alleviate conflict between farmers and predators," he said, morphing back into semi-human form. "We need to understand the role of predators in ecosystems. The Cape Leopard Trust is actually more about broader environmental conservation. We're using leopards as our sexy flagship species for a much bigger project."

By now I was hugging myself to keep warm and my lips had turned blue. I tried not to ask any more questions so he'd hurry up and stop acting like a suspicious leopard and we could go home.

"You see, many farmers, and even the Department of Agriculture, ignore the fact that when you kill the apex predators others simply move in. If you do somehow manage to eliminate all of them, another species will fill the gap and could bring with it even bigger problems. For instance, if you knock off all the leopards in one area, you might get a population explosion of dassies. The apex predators keep everything in balance. So the future must be about livestock management, not predator destruction."

"Gets a bit ch-ch-chilly up here when the s-s-sun goes down," I managed to say.

"Are you getting cold?"

"I-I-I think…"

"Look, we need to maintain functioning eco-systems." Quinton wasn't interested in my discomfort. "The trust is conducting experiments with sheep farming in the Northern Cape. We're using trained herders and special dogs. The herders gather all sorts of info on both the livestock and the predators. This way we can make farming more scientific and offer concrete results to the naysayers."

"Um, I think I m-m-might need to head back to the ve-ve-ve-hicle before hypothermia sets in."

"We want to do more studies on baboon, caracal and jackal. Also klipspringer and dassie, to see how the whole ecosystem fits together. And to find ways of alleviating farmer-predator conflict."

I began swinging my arms around like a windmill, hoping centrifugal force would return some blood to my hands. Eventually Quinton was done. He stood up, brushed the sand from his knees and took off the gardening gloves he'd put on to set the trap. Apart from the red flag and warning signs, it was impossible to see that the path hid a trap. Quinton loaded the equipment into his backpack, handed me the spade, and we trudged down the valley. Ahead of us, the sun's last rays illuminated Tafelberg. Its highest ramparts glowed in ethereal shades of salmon; the rest of the valley was sunk in deep shadow.

Quinton dropped me back at my hut and headed to his home deeper in the mountains at Matjiesrivier. I donned three extra layers and lit a *braai* fire. The wind was sniping and low clouds poured in from the west over Middelberg. I opened a bottle of workmanlike Shiraz and sat beside the fire, staring at the living darkness. There was no moon and the stars hissed quietly in the icy firmament. The stream grumbled loudly, wind whooshed in the bare branches, the black mountains pressed closer. Somewhere, close by, was my leopard. She was up there among the crags, perhaps hunting, perhaps taking refuge from the elements beneath an overhang. Maybe, just maybe, she was watching. A prickle of excitement coursed through me.

Sitting beside the pyramid of flames I thought about how the Cape Mountain Leopard had become a creature of legend and a symbol of what the Cape has lost. Three and a half centuries ago, when Jan van Riebeeck stepped ashore to found his little Dutch colony, the peninsula teemed with game. Cape Town itself was home to the 'Big Five.' There were leopard on the crags of Table Mountain, buffalo and rhino grazing the marshlands of Green Point, lion in Oranjezicht and elephant browsing along the streams within the city, while the grunts of hippo echoed round the City Bowl. It was an Eden of almost unimaginable bounty.

Settlers and farmers soon began to clear the land of wild animals. The hippo in Cape Town's rivers were among of the first to be shot. By the end of the 20th century there was not a single member of the Big Five left on the peninsula. The slaughter of big game continued throughout the Western Cape. In most places, it's only the names of geographical locations that remind us of what we have lost: Zeekoevlei (hippo lagoon), Buffels Bay (buffalo bay), Renosterveld (rhinoceros veld), Leeukloof (lion gorge), Olifants River (elephant river). Most prevalent is the name 'tier' or 'tyger.' Early Dutch settlers, unfamiliar with wild African fauna, called the leopards they encountered 'tigers.' Travelling among Cape mountains, it's never long before you come across a Tygerberg or Tierkop, a Tierberg or Tierkranskop. Of all the Cape's free-roaming game it was these secretive creatures that had the best chance of surviving into the 21st century. Their ghostly presence in the mountains fringing the city is a reminder of the rich diversity of wildlife that has been lost.

After a meal of *wors*, chops, and potato in a skin of tinfoil I climbed into an icy bed piled with blankets. Sleep came quickly... and I found myself stumbling along a track in the mountains. There was no moon to light the way, only a softening of the darkness that marked a sandy path. I was frightened. The rocky crags breathed danger.

Crickets filled the night with their threatening song. There was a presence, something watching me. Perhaps the spotted night cat, prince of darkness. My path snaked into a narrow *kloof* towards a stream. Tall reeds pressed in from either side. The ground was soggy underfoot; my legs grew leaden. I passed beneath a gnarled cedar tree and paused. Big boughs blotted out the stars. Fear gripped me. I couldn't take another step.

Glancing up, I saw a shape draped on a branch above my head. He was looking down, a pair of golden eyes boring into me. His mouth was partly open and I could see white fangs. What beauty, what lethal grace. I was transfixed. 'Tyger! Tyger! Burning bright' in the mountains of the night. He was all power and sinew and dark fire, a work of art crafted by some immortal hand. He stared at me for what seemed an age, each second painfully torn from the flesh of time. Then he simply closed his eyes and rested his chin on those mighty paws. I walked on into the night feeling more alive than ever I could remember.

CHAPTER THREE

The search for Max

The rusty hinges of guinea fowl woke me early, followed by utter silence. I got up and looked out of the window. The ground was white with frost. The mountains were colorful cut-outs against a dark blue sky. A Hadeda Ibis strutted about looking officious and drilling the lawn with its beak for nibbles. Quinton arrived to collect me after breakfast. We picked up Garth and Lorraine and headed down the Driehoek Valley in search of Max. Gracie stayed behind to hold the fort: with her biting tongue she'd certainly scare off most intruders, except, perhaps, a spotted cat.

Quinton soon picked up a good signal coming from the male leopard's collar on Sneeuberg, the 6650 foot massif to our right. Fortunately, he had a key to a private gate that let us onto a forestry track that wound up a spectacular valley towards the peak. We crossed a stream and ploughed through tall vegetation whose fingers brushed the sides of the 4x4. The track grew steeper and more bouldery. On a rise above us stood a line of the Cederberg's iconic cedar trees, highly endangered and probably on their way to extinction. Prone to fire and ruthlessly felled for timber in the 20th century, only a few specimens cling on in the high berg. Two black eagles circled above us like patrolling aircraft, their menacing shapes etched against the sky. Like leopards, these are apex predators of the berg and there's no love lost between cat and bird as they compete for the same prey. Whenever eagles get the chance, they dive bomb leopards to scare them from their territory.

We drew to a halt at what looked like a stone igloo beside the road. There was a narrow entrance and a metal sliding door that could be triggered to drop like a guillotine and imprison a creature inside. It was a sinister contraption, casting a pall over the fynbos beauty around us.

"This is an old leopard trap," said Quinton. "All the farms in the area used to have them. Some are more than 150 years old. Once the creature was caught, you could shoot it from above, through gaps in the stonework. Farmers knew exactly where to place these things. So, I've put many of my own traps around here and had good success."

He explained further that gin traps are nasty devices still used extensively throughout South Africa to eliminate 'problem animals.' Thousands litter the rural landscape. They are indiscriminate and kill or maim far more innocent animals than rogues. Usually made of metal with saw-tooth jaws, the traps can sever a paw or ensnare the wounded animal long enough for it to starve to death. "We are making progress, though, especially in the Cederberg. I've persuaded many farmers to change their methods, like introducing Anatolian sheep dogs. It's a far better deterrent than traps.

"Look there!" he exclaimed and crouched next to the track, pointing at a vague indentation in the sand. He took a tape measure from his bag. "Paw print. Two-and-a-half inches. Female. I'm sure it's F11. We haven't caught and collared her yet, so she doesn't have a proper name."

We walked a little way up the slope following the spoor. Quinton pointed at the ground again. It was animal droppings, known as 'scat.' It's difficult for lay people to fathom the excitement scat induces in zoologists. Quinton fell to his knees like a worshipper and studied the specimen closely. He explained that usually only half the scat is taken for analysis, as it serves as a territory marker for leopards. Samples are soaked in formalin, washed, and the hair separated from other remains before the sample is oven dried at 140°F.

Then the analysis can begin. To identify prey, the hair length and color is noted, as well as cuticular hair-scale patterns. The presence of bone fragments and hooves also aids identification. Small rodents are more difficult to identify, although teeth found in the scat can help. Quinton explained that through scat research he'd recorded 23 species in the diet of these opportunistic feeders, including everything from lizard to cow. I thought of the many hours he had spent soaking scat in formalin and baking it and then the days spent examining it. This kind of dedication needs to be fed by a particular brand of obsession.

We pressed on up the pass, switchbacking on increasingly precipitous bends, creeping along the mountain face on a hairline track that led us into a world of jumbled sandstone and bright green fynbos. Clouds cast giant dapples across the valley. All the while the bleating transmission from Max's collar grew more intense. At the top of the pass we got out and Quinton aimed his VHF telemetry at a nearby *koppie*. The signal was strong. He switched to a UHF aerial and got a GPS fix from the collar. Max was 930 yards to the west, just this side of a tall ridge. The four of us spent a few minutes scanning the area with binoculars, but saw nothing. Every bush and boulder looked vaguely feline.

Every feature in the landscape seemed ideal camouflage for a leopard.

"Okay, we're going to have to hike in after him," said Quinton. "It could be a bit rough."

The two retirees opted out, saying they'd rather sit and look at the view. Out came folding chairs and a flask of coffee. Knowing a wild goose chase when I saw one, I half wanted to join them. But I'd come to the berg to bag a leopard and this was as good a shot as any. Hats, water bottles, telemetry, binoculars — we were good to go.

Quinton uses telemetry to track the collared male leopard Max on the slopes of Sneeuberg.

Ahead of us lay difficult terrain: a salad of rocks that had been sliced and diced into awkward shapes. Quinton set off at a cracking pace. He has long legs and is used to pursuing feline quarry in the mountains. I have city legs, made for strolling the promenade as far as my local coffee bar. My lack of fitness became painfully apparent about a minute into our pursuit. Quinton was like a Zen walker who never actually touched the ground. His patent leather Caterpillar hooves were like wings; my old *velskoens* like anchors. I puffed and wheezed in his wake. Where his long strides propelled him over gaps, I found myself caught between them. While his breathing remained even, I sounded like a steam engine.

He crouched down behind a pile of stones up ahead. I made a last push, using all my reserves of strength to catch up. He glanced back with a frown and put a finger to his lips. I flopped down beside him, heaving like a turtle that had just lugged its hefty body up a beach. Sweat poured off me. I was red as a tomato. Quinton might have had a drop of perspiration on his brow. We had covered at least 550, near-vertical yards. He poked the telemetry aerial above the ledge like a periscope. Max had to be very close. There was no signal whatsoever, only a hissing sound.

"Shit, the bugger's gone over the edge," whispered Quinton. "Might have got wind of us. Come on!"

We were off, bounding up the slope to the next ridge line. The weather began closing in. Clouds scudded through saw-tooth gaps in the berg. The wind turned icy and the towering Sneeuberg dissolved into white. It began to rain. Quinton was pulling ahead once more. I watched him stop and stare at the terrain, head to one side, thinking like a cat again. Which way would Max have gone? Then the half-man, half-leopard slunk over a rise and disappeared.

After half an hour we reached another ridge line. I collapsed next to Quinton, wheezing like a rasp. My thighs were incendiary and my right knee, the dickey one, had sort of capitulated. My vision was all spots and floaty hallucinogens. A leopard could have been standing six feet away and I'd have dismissed it as retina malfunction.

Quinton raised his telemetry aerial. "I've got a faint signal. Could be bouncing off the cliff. Max is heading west. He's missioning. We'll never catch him. This is the easternmost part of his range. He could be gone for weeks now, prowling his territory along the western slopes of the berg. It's completely inaccessible. I'm sorry."

We headed back, making a detour to a spot where Max had recently made a kill. All that remained was a bed of klipspringer fur, which had been carefully plucked by the leopard, and a reeking pile of stomach contents. Everything else had been consumed.

"From the data we got from his GPS collar we know Max spent about 24 hours on this carcass," said Quinton. "When we notice a GPS cluster in one particular spot we come and investigate as it's likely to be a kill. These cats are so mobile, when they're stationary for a while it usually means they're feeding. But we missed him by about an hour. Such a sneaky fellow is our Max."

Bushnell   08-06-2010 12:28

Max triggers a camera trap high in the Cederberg with the flat-topped Tafelberg (1969 metres) in the background.

CHAPTER FOUR

Winning hearts and minds

That evening, Quinton was due to give a talk on leopards at Mount Cedar, a popular lodge in a nearby valley. I got a lift with Garth and Lorraine to Quinton's home in Matjiesrivier, a lovely thatched house leased from Cape Nature, where he lives with his wife Elizabeth. She's a willowy Pre-Raphaelite looking woman with a mane of curly auburn hair and a Julia Roberts smile. Elizabeth, once a teacher at a Waldorf school in Stellenbosch, today runs environmental education and wilderness camps for children at Matjiesrivier. The house serves as the de facto headquarters of the Cape Leopard Trust. The high-ceilinged, creaky rooms are crammed with zoological books, pictures of big cats and maps of their distribution: it is the home of working scientists.

We transferred to Quinton's vehicle for the drive to Mount Cedar. Night was falling and the mountains were at their most seductive. The rocks turned from gold to purple to burnished black and stars began to prickle the dusky sky. Nearing Mount Cedar, we breasted a rise and Quinton said:

"This is exactly where I saw my first leopard. I'd been searching for nearly a year by then, and suddenly there it was, caught in my headlights. Just the briefest glimpse, but it was electrifying."

He told us about his early searches in the desolate Karoo Cederberg to the east of the road we were driving. "It's the most isolated part of the mountains. No-one ever goes there. That's why I love it so much. You can walk for days and not see any sign of man. Pure wilderness. I was in the leopards' environment, alone, sleeping wild. Occasionally I'd be backtracking along a route I'd just walked and there'd be fresh leopard spoor across my path. They knew all about my presence. I'd often hear other animals alarm calling. The leopards were close. But never so much as a glimpse. Just knowing they were there was enough, though. *Not* seeing them made it even more special, if you get my drift. The invisible cats."

We arrived at Mount Cedar for Quinton's 6:30 pm presentation to a bunch of wealthy tourists. There were possible sponsors among them, so Quinton had been persuaded by the tour leader to do his 'song and dance routine.' But there was no-one in the auditorium and at Mount Cedar dinner is served at 7 pm sharp. Quinton has to be a patient man, content to wait months for the glimpse of a cat. Now we witnessed his less patient side –I could almost see smoke coming out of his ears. He'd been specially asked to come here. It was a favor. Dinner would just have to wait, or there'd be hell to pay.

Eventually, a group of well-heeled mountain bikers sauntered in, chatting and laughing loudly among themselves. There were carefully groomed women and blustery men accompanied by much bravado and bonhomie. I thought Quinton might lose his temper, but the moment he began his talk he was charm personified and the audience soon settled down and warmed to him. Elizabeth turned down the lights and images flashed on a screen. He'd done the PowerPoint presentation countless times before and was completely at ease with his material.

We learnt about how, after 350 years of farmer-predator strife, most of the Western Cape's rich wildlife biodiversity had disappeared. The last big cats, hanging on in a few scraps of wilderness, were all that was left. When Quinton founded the trust in 2004 an average of eight leopards were being shot in the Cederberg each year. Since 2004 only two had been killed.

He explained that the Cape Leopard was an 'umbrella species,' used as an emblem for research on the whole ecosystem and for environmental education. The tools of Quinton's trade were simple. Feet on the ground were the most important element, since much of the terrain was inaccessible by vehicle. Infrared camera traps were vital, as they provided permanent eyes and could be used to identify individual leopards (their distinctive pattern of spots being the equivalent of a fingerprint). Also essential were the traps to capture animals, allowing researchers to attach GPS collars.

Quinton showed various maps depicting the ranges of his collared cats. He'd found that in the mountains male leopard ranges were up to 75 square miles, compared to the Karoo, where ranges were as high as 450 square miles or the densely populated Kruger National Park, where they were as low as 10 square miles. He'd recorded how ranges changed over time as cats were forced out or died. His leopards cover up to 18 miles a day, patrolling their territory, hunting and looking for mates. Only one male holds any given patch, although you might find a couple of females and young cats overlapping.

Pointing to bunches of dots on the maps, depicting GPS clusters, he explained that these indicated where a leopard had made a kill. Visits to these sites had enabled an accurate picture of their diet to be put together. A pie chart showed a menu comprising of 44% klipspringer, 34% dassie and 3% livestock, with the remainder made up of a wide range of creatures in very small quantities.

He stressed that his research had proved that farm animals comprised a negligible part of a leopard's diet. The key to eliminating that portion completely was livestock management. He spoke about his project in Namaqualand where eco-ranger herders with Anatolian sheep dogs were doing pioneering work with sheep flocks. Employing herders and dogs and placing livestock in a *kraal* at night almost entirely eradicated predation. It simply required a mind shift by farmers.

Quinton then showed photographs from his infrared camera traps. They depicted the wide biodiversity of the berg, from porcupine and honey badger to caracal and baboon. Next came an image of two leopard cubs frolicking, which had the audience ah-ing. "These little beauties were born on 7 January 2011," said Quinton. "Both have survived and dispersed into the mountains."

Infrared camera traps work 24 hours a day. Individual leopards are identified by the pattern of their spots, much like human fingerprints.

When his talk ended the audience had plenty of questions.

How much did mountain leopards weigh?

Answer: males were about 78 lb on average, which was half that of their cousins elsewhere in Africa.

Were Cape Mountain Leopards a sub-species in their own right?

Answer: probably not, although more research had to be done to determine this. However, one feature that distinguished them from other leopards was a black rather than a pink nose.

How many Cape Leopards were left?

Answer: about 30 adults in the Cederberg and possibly 400 in total. It is a terribly fragile population. An outbreak of disease, such as feline AIDS, could wipe them all out.

Were there any left on Table Mountain or the Cape peninsula?

Answer: no, although many hikers had reported otherwise. Quinton would have to be shown photographs to be convinced. The range around Cape Town had shrunk to unsustainable proportions. "You'd find Constantia poodles and Boulders Beach penguins getting nailed if they were still around," said Quinton. "We must assume that peninsula leopards are extinct."

The applause was loud and long. The tour-group leader stood up to thank Quinton and told the audience the Cape Leopard Trust only survived on donations. Would they please give generously. As we packed up, the leader came to tell us that a number of his guests would be dipping into their purses for the cause. Our trip had not been in vain.

"Fund raising and PR are a huge part of the job," said Quinton as we drove back. "I'd love to be on my own in the berg tracking leopards full time, but it's just not possible anymore. The Trust is a big organization with staff and responsibilities. We have projects all over the Cape, investors to keep satisfied and the interested public needs to be kept informed about all our activities."

We stopped for supper at Matjiesrivier. Around the *braai*, talk was all about the elusive nature of Cape Leopards. Quinton had worked for years at Londolozi Game Reserve, where leopards were spotted on almost every game drive. Later, he'd worked at a number of Wilderness Safaris camps in Botswana, where leopards were also fairly easy to spot. He'd recently visited Phinda Game Reserve in KwaZulu-Natal, to compare notes with researchers who used similar trapping methods. Before they'd even set the last of a series of snares the first one had been triggered by an inquisitive leopard. In the Cederberg you could wait half a year for that.

"So, why on earth do you do it?" I asked.

"Part of the mystery is their elusiveness. In the Cape, leopards have become mystical beasts. I like that about them. I'm not generally a patient man..."

"You can say that again," chirped Elizabeth.

"… but I make an exception with leopards. I have to."

Elizabeth told us about the time they had had a television crew staying with them for a month, desperate for a sighting. Quinton stared sheepishly into his beer as his wife recounted the incident. Days dragged by and they had no luck. Finally one of the transmitters was triggered: a leopard had been caught in a cage trap high in the mountains. It took them hours to lug the heavy camera equipment up there. When they got close, the crew set up a shot looking down on the hidden trap. With the cameras rolling, Quinton carefully approached the cage, only to discover that the cat had managed to escape. At that moment, his patience gave out and with a roar of rage he picked up the cage and hurled it over a cliff, cameras rolling all the while. The TV crew got some lovely footage of an enraged man-leopard.

CHAPTER FIVE

"Herding cats"

The next day Lorraine and Garth had to return to the city to attend their grandchildren's school concert. Instead of Quinton having to dismantle the three traps while waiting for more volunteers to arrive I offered to take over monitoring. This involved checking the frequencies for each trap every couple of hours throughout the day and night. If the pulse doubled from its usual 40 beats a minute, a snare had been triggered and I was to summon Quinton on the satellite phone. We rigged up an aerial on the roof of my hut and led the cable through a window so the receiver could reach my bedside table. That way, I wouldn't have to get up in the night to check the signal.

"If the trap is sprung, I'll go in alone and assess the situation from a distance," said Quinton. "I don't want you with me at that point. Approaching an angry cat can be pretty terrifying. I was stalked by a leopard once in Londolozi. There's nothing quite like that primal fear."

I imagined a writhing, spitting ball of teeth and claws on the end of a wire and agreed that it would probably be best if I came later with the vets and their darting rifles.

For the rest of my time at Driehoek, I stayed close to the receiver. I took the occasional stroll around the farm or along the lower slopes of Corridor Peak behind the homestead, but felt responsible for the traps. I didn't want a leopard to spend any longer than was necessary with its paw in a noose. All frequencies, however, continued to bleat a negative. I set my alarm clock to sound at intervals during the night. Each time I woke to check the receiver there'd be a thrill of expectation. It was like spinning a roulette wheel: this time I'd strike it lucky.

Days dragged by and I worried I might sit in that hut for many months with no reward. Besides, the city had begun to assert itself; first the odd SMS, then phone calls: bills, the plumber, a body corporate meeting. On my last day in the mountains, Quinton and Elizabeth arrived to take me on a hunt for Spot, the female that frequented our area. It was a final roll of the dice.

While driving up Uilsgat Kloof we picked up a strong telemetry signal. She was definitely in the valley. But where? Her echo bounced off the rocky walls, making accurate bearings difficult. We parked and got out.

"I'm getting a fairly good signal from the other side of the *kloof*, half way up Mied se Berg," said Quinton. "You okay for a bit of a hike?"

"Sure thing," I said unconvincingly. By now, I knew what 'a bit of a hike' meant.

As we prepared our packs with water, food, cameras, binoculars and telemetry equipment, Elizabeth happened to glance at the cliff and exclaimed: "Look at those black eagles! They're dive bombing something!"

"My God, I'll bet you its Spot," said Quinton, grabbing his binoculars.

We watched the two great birds making an attack run. They approached in a parabolic swoop, then folded their wings and dropped out of the sky in a near vertical dive. As they plummeted each bird let out a bloodcurdling scream that raised the hairs on the back of my neck. The Stuka dive bombers of the berg. At the last moment, when it seemed inevitable the birds would smash themselves against the cliff in an explosion of feathers, they flared their enormous wings and pulled out, talons extended, almost brushing the rock as they soared back into the blue.

"There, on that big boulder, she's cowering!" shouted Quinton.

I trained my binoculars in the direction he was pointing. Nothing. Or perhaps a glimpse of movement?

"Where exactly?" I asked.

"The big round rock, above the diagonal one."

I looked again, willing the leopard to show itself. Which round rock, which diagonal one? They were all round or diagonal. There! Had I seen something? Maybe just the hint of cat, a vague feline suggestion? Maybe not.

"She must have slipped behind it," said Quinton. "Let's move. Fast. If we angle to the left we can herd her up the valley towards our traps and maybe get a sighting into the bargain."

"Herding cats," I muttered under my breath as we set off across the valley floor at an unsustainable pace. Quinton and Elizabeth took giraffe strides; mine were more modest. We came to a stream and my two companions appeared to step over it without changing their stride. I sloshed through, filling my shoes with mud. By now, every animal in the valley knew about Spot, and the alarm calls of a grey rhebok ahead of us were picked up by a troop of baboons behind. The *kloof* was a natural amphitheater and the sounds echoed about us, backed by a chorus of birdsong. I was thrilled. It was just like being Richard Attenborough in the climactic scene of a BBC documentary.

We scaled the western slope and veered along a contour towards the boulder. My two companions had changed from giraffes to klipspringers, their cloven hoofs gripping the rocks as they gamboled ahead. I slipped, grazing a knee. The telemetry, pinging like sonar, told us Spot hadn't moved far and Quinton motioned us to continue in complete silence.

We came to a rocky outcrop, took off our packs and scrambled up to a ledge. My shoes sent a pebble clip-clopping down the valley. Quinton looked back with a severe frown. Poking our heads over the edge, we scanned the area where Spot should have been. The telemetry told us she was less than 50 yards away but invisible to us. The dassies on a nearby boulder were going ballistic with their alarm calls: they had certainly seen her. All we could do was wait for Spot to show herself.

This waiting and staring and telemetrying and looking at each other with quizzical looks went on for about 20 minutes. Then Quinton edged off to the left and we followed, trying not to dislodge stones or breathe too loudly.

"She's on the move," whispered Quinton. "You two wait here. I'll try to flush her out."

He scrambled down the rock face, angling to the right to force her up the valley and into open ground. His telemetry aerial swung back and forth above his head, making him look like a robot-man. We scanned the scrub, triangulating our gaze with the direction of Quinton's aerial. How could a big cat vanish in broad daylight with such meager cover, right under our noses, and wearing a telemetry collar to boot?

After half an hour, Quinton returned, looking dejected. We found some shade and ate our sandwiches. "As you can see, this is a very frustrating game," he said, staring across the valley to where the baboon troop was barking loudly, marking Spot's progress somewhere up the opposite slope.

CHAPTER SIX

A sort of spotting of Spot

My time was up. I drove out of the enchanted valley, over Uitkyk Pass, and down the snaking gravel road to Algeria. My thoughts turned to how, up there in the mountains, the future of leopards is relatively secure. For now, at least. In 2007 a 660 mi² area was set aside as the Cederberg Conservancy. At Quinton's urging, the entire farming community had agreed to ban gin traps. Livestock farming with sheep, goats and cattle had, until then, been the predominant land use; now olives, citrus and wine production predominated. Leopards are not vegetarians... and they're teetotalers.

And what of Spot? Had I seen her or hadn't I? My imagination had certainly produced a vision of sorts. Spot was there on the rock, bathed in sunshine, her back arched. She was staring up at the great bird falling towards her. Her whiskers bristled as she bared her fangs. Those golden eyes, their pupils narrowed to tiny slits, measured the approach of the eagle, readying to strike if it came close enough. A flicking tail, claws anchoring her to the rock, a camouflaged body pressed low. I could even hear the low growl coming from deep inside her, like the sound of distant thunder.

Had I seen her? Quinton certainly had. Elizabeth might have caught a glimpse. I was less sure. Did the fact that one person in the group achieved a sighting mean that, technically, the group as a whole had seen a leopard? Is one's own, personal pair of flawed, short-sighted eyes that important in the bigger scheme of 'the sighting?'

And maybe I had, actually, seen a fleeting spotted shape of sorts. A half-sighting or perhaps a 'sort of' sighting. Did a half-sighting count as a sighting? If one rounded the half up to a whole, which even the most fastidious accountants are wont to do, then I had definitely spotted Spot. I *had* seen a Cape Mountain Leopard! Sort of.

UNSPOTTED

About the Author

Justin Fox is a travel writer, novelist and editor based in Cape Town. He was a Rhodes Scholar and received a doctorate in English from Oxford University after which he became a research fellow at the University of Cape Town, where he now teaches part time. His articles and photographs have appeared internationally in a number of publications and on a wide range of topics, while his short stories and poems have appeared in various anthologies. He is a two-time Mondi journalism award winner (1999 and 2004). His recent books include *The Marginal Safari* (Umuzi, 2010), nominated for the 2011 Alan Paton Award for non-fiction and the 2012 Olive Schreiner Prize for Literature, and a not-so-swashbuckling pirate novel, *Whoever Fears the Sea* (Umuzi, 2014), longlisted for the Etisalat Prize for Literature. Find Justin online at justinfoxafrica.wordpress.com and on Facebook as JustinFoxAuthor.

About the Publisher

Annorlunda Books is a small press that publishes books to inform, entertain, and make you think. We publish short books (novella length or shorter) and collections of short writing, fiction and non-fiction.

Find more information about us and our books online: annorlundaenterprises.com/books or on Twitter: @AnnorlundaInc.

To stay up to date on all of our releases, subscribe to our mailing list at:

annorlundaenterprises.com/mailing-list

Other Titles from Annorlunda Books

Short eBooks

Caresaway, by DJ Cockburn, is a near-future thriller about a man who discovers a drug to cure depression, but finds that the wonder drug comes at great cost to himself... and the world.

The Lilies of Dawn, by Vanessa Fogg, is a lyrical fantasy novelette about love, duty, family, and one young woman's coming of age.

Okay, So Look, by Micah Edwards, is a humorous, yet accurate and thought-provoking, retelling of the Book of Genesis.

Navigating the Path to Industry, by M.R. Nelson, is a hiring manager's advice on how to run a successful non-academic job search.

Don't Call It Bollywood, by Margaret E. Redlich, is an introduction to the world of Hindi film.

Collections

Missed Chances is a Taster Flight collection of classic stories about love, all with a hint of "the one that got away."

Love and Other Happy Endings is another Taster Flight of classic stories, all of which end on a high note.

Small and Spooky is a Taster Flight of classic ghost stories, all of which feature a child.

Academaze, by Sydney Phlox, is a collection of essays and cartoons about life in academia.